For All I Know

For All I Know

Poems by

J. R. Solonche

Cover design by Shay Culligan

ISBN: 978-1-950462-72-8

Kelsay Books
502 S 1040 E, A-119
American Fork, Utah, 84003

Books by this Author

Enjoy Yourself
To Say the Least
The Porch Poems
The Time of Your Life
True Enough
In a Public Place
If You Should See Me Walking on the Road
The Jewish Dancing Master
Tomorrow, Today, and Yesterday
In Short Order
I, Emily Dickinson and Other Found Poems
Invisible
Won't Be Long
Heart's Contest
The Black Birch
Beautiful Day
Peach Girl: Poems for a Chinese Daughter (with Joan I. Siegel)

Acknowledgments

The Atticus Review: "Hammock," "I Asked the Man Mowing"

The Flask Review: "Gorge"

Into the Teeth of the Wind: "Listening to Bach While Driving in Early March"

The Lake: "Poetry"

The Magnolia Review: "For a Friend Who Wanted to Hear the Music Better," "Lying on My Back," "Winter Afternoon"

Offcourse: A Literary Journal: "Cheap Red Wine," "Cutty Sark," "Linda's Office Supply," "Sermon on the Balcony," "The Practice"

One Sentence Poems: "After a Chinese Poem," "The Passenger Jet"

Otis Nebula: "Haiku for Solo Piano"

Under a Warm Green Linden: "The Wind"

Contents

Part II: Ghazal-Sonnets

Part III

Part I

How Strange That Nothing Anymore Seems Strange

The wind has died down.
The branches are still once more.
The clouds have disappeared into the arms of the night.

The poem I was reading returns to the page.
The page goes back to the book.
The book finds its place on the shelf where it was.

The shelf becomes one wall of the room again.
The room gathers the house around its shoulders.
The house, relieved of duties, sighs a sigh of relief.

This would be the perfect place for a question.
I do not know any questions.
For this I am grateful.

I have forgotten what questions are for.
Let us celebrate the absence of answers.
Let us say, *Amen, Amen* to the absence of answers.

A dream awaits me.
I see it waiting patiently at the window.
It has been there reading a poem about itself a long time.

The dream is nodding its head in approval.
It is humming softly so as not to wake me.
It pretends not to be wise, for it pretends to be me.

Poetry

"I like your poem," I told the student.
"It's really good." "Thanks," she said.
"You should publish more," I said.
"I don't have any more right now,"
she said. "I'm very hard on myself."
"That's good," I said. "Being hard on
yourself is the best way to be. It will
make things a lot easier later on.
You'll see." I'm such a fucking liar.
Not about the poem. The poem really
was good. About the later on part.

December

The lake is freezing over,
but whose voice is that?

Is it the voice of the ice
or the voice of the water?

Autumn Afternoon

I hear it every day these days,
the sound of my neighbor's chainsaw

cutting up the dead trees
behind his house to burn through the winter.

It is the sound of a starving animal gorging on its kill.
I can see the white smoke

like the ghosts of the trees swarming from the chimney,
coming up for air.

When I go outside with the trash or to fill the bird feeder with seed,
I can smell the smoke.

It fills my lungs.
I choke on it.

I know full well that these are trees burning, just trees.
Nevertheless, I look away.

Listening to Bach While Driving in Early March

Where the road uncurves between
the two cornfields a straight and level
three quarters of a mile, I let go
of the wheel to open the window,
to tap the rhythm out on my lap
with my palms. I want the world
to hear this harpsichord shout over
the trees beyond the fields. I want
the world to hear these violins string
psalms down the power lines.
I want the world to hear these flutes
like silver-throated birds returning
from the south. Will anything ever
make more sense than this? Nothing
will ever make more sense than this.
Nothing from my mouth or from
anyone else's will ever make more
sense than this. I pass a father teaching
his son to ride his new bicycle. He is
teaching him to keep his balance on
the narrow wheels, his hands on the bars
tight, going fast downhill, the father
alongside. Something else has to happen,
I think. Something else, now or very soon,
has to happen, I think, or a hundred
mornings will fall off my life to balance
this morning of Bach and of glory.

After the Rehearsal

Wind drives leaves across the road.
Mozart's *Requiem* remains in my mind's ear.
It remains in my ear's mind and has become a tree of human
voices.

The wind drives the leaves across the road, ahead, in my car's
beam.
I hear the tree of voices die.
I hear it fall away voice by voice in the wind.

The tree is bare but for the boom of one last leaf-voice.
Then that, too, joins the wind as I open the door of the laundry
room.

Baudelaire

The eyes are more than eyes.
The smile is less than a smile.
The forehead is high and the hair wispy thin.

The mouth has the shape of cruelty
but is not cruel really since it lacks guile.
The lips have kissed too much perhaps.

On his mind is a glass of port wine,
an unpaid bill, art, and the stars
like salt on the black wound of his heart.

The Feminist Poet

Don't you see her red tongue wag?
Isn't it just like lewd laundry?

And her nipples, aren't they like the tips of ballpoint pens?
Don't you get bitten by the zipper of her lines?

Doesn't your mind catch and run?
Don't you, too, want to run?

For a Friend Who Wants to Hear the Music Better

Okay, stand on what ledge?
On what hilltop?
On what foothold
on the edge

of leverage?
Where is
the chair
closer to the stage?

And where
is the music
anyway if
not everywhere?

The universe
has no orchestra,
no choir,
no soloist,

only the ping
of particles,
the cosmic chatter,
background noise of Nothing.

Are these the harps?
Are these the wings
of angels? Are these
the flats and sharps

of the Music Spherical?
Here, only here,
is the trapdoor stage.
Dance, friend, so dance on it well.

What They Will Say

One will say I take my identity
from whatever is at hand.
It is not difficult to be stony and silent as the moon
is silent and stony.
It is not difficult to be a mirror, either full or empty.

One will say I know as well as anyone how things
ought to be and ought not to be.
It is not difficult to follow instruction if it is clear.
My eye as well is fine, and my hand as well is firm
and steady on the wheel.

One will say when I walked on the road at dusk,
I saw everything there was to see.
Although now I have forgotten most of what I saw,
I still remember the branches of the oaks
thrashing themselves like penitents.

One will say it is not difficult to forget when I want to.
Even childhood falls off one day like a rotten limb.
Even love leaves no trace sometimes as it passes
Even love leaves no trace sometimes as it passes, one will say.

Lilies of the Valley

Little
wedding bells
for
little weddings.

Little
marriage bells
for little brides
and little bridegrooms.

Lilies of the Valley,
you are not
serious flowers,
and I

cannot take
you seriously
therefore.
There is

something funny
about you,
something quite
comical,

something
I cannot
take seriously.
Eight, nine

ten tiny
wedding bells
for weddings
the size of

Lilies of the Valley.
Eight, nine, ten
little bells,
little comical bells.

Lying on My Back on the Bench

Lying on my back on the bench
behind the house, looking up at the black
and gold branches of the black birch tree
against the perfect blue perfect clear
perfect sky, the newspaper of April
twenty-fourth on the ground,
wherein disgust for that which I read
on the front page, and in awe for
that which I read on the second page,
I dropped it beside me, I understand
man's cruelty and the acts of violence
that men commit, without sense, against
one another and against all life,
and I understand the cold unblinking stare
of man's science as it stares into the cold
unblinking stare of the universe's science,
but I do not understand the beauty of the world,
not the cold, cold unblinking beauty of the world.

The Painting *Mi Fu Bowing to Elder Brother Stone* by Yu Ming

Mi Fu by bowing has made
a rock of himself.

Elder Brother Stone by being
bowed to does not change.

The space between
Mi Fu and Elder

Brother Stone,
however, changes.

After a Chinese Poem

Not eager for news, I am the recluse
who will not answer the door for fear
he will open to one who comes this near
only to ask the way to another's house.

A Man Sits in a World of Sunshine and Lilies

A man sits in a world of sunshine and lilies.
A newspaper is in his lap.
In the newspaper is a world of smoke and blood.
He does not know which one is real.
A woman sits in the world of smoke and blood.
No newspaper is in her lap.
There is no world of sunshine and lilies for her to see.
She needs not wonder which one is real.
She knows the world of smoke and blood is real.
She knows the smoke is real.
It is in her lungs.
She knows the blood is real.
It is on her hands.
She knows her scream is real.
It is the voices of her mother and her mother's mother.
It is her voice three times over.
She knows her pain is real.
It tastes of her own heart.
She knows any other world is not real.
She knows any other world is a dream.
She knows there is no such place as a world of sunshine and lilies.
The lilies turn black in his lungs.
The sunshine turns red on his hands.

Ground Zero

It is zero ground.
It is ground minus.
It is ground ungrounded.
It is ground ground down to below ground.

Tell me it is larger than the hole we dig in the ground for the tulip.
Tell me it is larger than the hole we dig in the ground for the corn
    plant.
Tell me it is larger than the hole we dig in the ground for the dead
    one.

I will tell you it is not as large as the holes we dig in the rainforest
    for the cattle.
I will tell you it is not as large as the holes we dig in the oceans for
    the toxins.
I will tell you it is not as large as the holes we dig in the sky for the
    poisons.

Most of all, I will tell you it is not as large as the hole we
dig in ourselves for the single mustard seed of zero.

I Asked the Man Mowing

I asked the man mowing
the grass in the cemetery
what it was like to mow grass
in a cemetery. "Come on
over and see for yourself,"
he said. I walked through
the gate. "Just be careful
not to swipe the stones.
Families get really upset
if you chip the stones,"
he said. I mowed a little,
enough to see for myself
what it was like to mow
grass in a cemetery. "Thanks,"
I said. "So?" he said. "So,
it was sorta weird," I said.
"Spooky, you know? Kind
of like I was giving a haircut
to the dead," I said. "It's just
another lawn job," he said.
"Except for them stones. Man,
the families really get pissed
when you hit them stones."

On the Message Machine

She wanted to know
what would be

the most appropriate
way to express condolence

to the neighbors' daughter
whose beloved pet dog

drowned in the family pool
while chasing a mouse,

and although I did not hear
my wife's advice and while certain

it was sensible, I would have asked
what happened to the mouse.

Honor

After listening, patiently, to all
the anti-war talk, he stood up.
He was my age. He said he was
a veteran of Vietnam. He said
he was still angry. He said he was
sick. He said he was still sick
after all these years. He said losing
the war made him sick, and he was
still sick over it. He said the peace
that ended the war was a bad peace.
He said it was a peace without honor.
He said he didn't want Iraq to end
the same way. He said he didn't
want to be sick a second time
over a war that ends badly, that
ends with a peace without honor.
He said we must stay and finish
the job. He said there must be honor.
Then he sat down. There was a long
silence. It wasn't long, but it felt
long. Then a man stood up. He was
our age. He could have been a vet
of Vietnam. He didn't say. He said,
calmly, quietly, almost inaudibly,
that for the Iraqis peace is enough.
He said, for you, my friend, honor is
enough. He said, so if that is all you
need, here. He handed him a slip of paper.
On the paper was written the word *Honor.*
Then he sat down. Then the veteran left.
Then the anti-war talk started up again.

Nature and Supernature

To fly fleet enough
from the natural
to arrive at the supernatural
means miracle's means.

A Triangle

A triangle
of light between
buildings.

A treasure
of concrete
lacquered and gilded

as cool as
the shadows
surrounding it

but in obverse
so the cool front
side of a shadow.

Three-sided rest
where the desperate
sunlight-mother

of a thousand
hungry children
goes to be alone.

Haiku for Solo Piano

The pianist in black
comes out, shakes hands with the piano.
They are attending the same funeral.

"The Steinway is dead,"
he said. "Wheel out the Yamaha
ha ha ha instead."

"The coffin of music,"
quipped James Joyce.
But listen, listen in living black and white.

The intermission:
Silent piano silent movie.
Unaccompanied.

The pianist in black
comes out, shakes hands with the piano.
They are going to play championship chess.

The huge black mouth,
nearly the size of the summer night.
"Listen," it says. "Here is a dream even longer than yours."

Short Speech for Adam

When I woke up
from that deep sleep,
I saw her there,
standing a few yards
away, in the shade
of two trees, with her
hands on her hips,
speaking to me in
the language of the hyenas.

The Book of Lilac

I have an idea for a book.
It will be a book of poems
about the lilac tree in my front
yard. Every poem in it will be
about the tree, and there will be
a hundred of them. The title
will be *The Book of Lilac.* Of
course, I will never write such
a book of a hundred poems
about the lilac in my front yard.
But I have written five or six,
so maybe with a little luck,
I won't have to write it to be
remembered for having written it.
Maybe someone a hundred years
from now will come across these
five or six poems and remember
a vague reference to a book entitled
The Book of Lilac and believe those
five or six poems were the only ones
not lost in the same dust in the same
corner of the same cellar of all lost books
of poetry. It is possible, with a little luck.

2:30 in the Morning

Rain
But it was not the rain that woke me.

Nor was it the wind that drove the rain against
the house. And it was not the crack and thud

of the dead tree falling in the woods across the road.
What woke me was the dream in which I tied

a rope around a larger-than-life statue of myself,
pulled with all my strength until the statue cracked

and fell to the ground with a heavy hollow thud.
I was awake, but the dream wasn't done.

I danced around it, clapping and singing.
O clapping, O and, O singing.

Perspective

Look long enough,
and it becomes flat.

The foreground of lake water,
the background of mountain,

then sky, change places.
In the middle distance,

the peninsula of pines
bleeds out its definition

in both directions. Look longer
and the vanishing point

vanishes, only to reappear
as the point of the church steeple,

which dreams,
in the dark,

when no one is looking,
of being a mountain.

At the Lake

There was one swan
on the lake

and one eagle
over the lake,

but because I did not know
which one to look at,

I looked at the space
between them.

Walking by the Marsh

Walking by the marsh,
I disturbed a hawk
but saved a field mouse
it had its eye on. How we
take sides just by being born.

The Big Brown Oak

leaf tumbled so
slowly down,
turned so
deliberately
while downward
over, I thought
it was a wren
showing off.

The Day Before

The day before
the swamp freezes
over, the black water
seizes the sun
and pulls it under.

After Dinner

After dinner,
I went for a walk.
A squirrel crossed
the road. I pointed
at it and said, "I will
never write a poem
about a squirrel."
Not because Eberhart
wrote the definitive one.
Not because Cinderella's
glass slipper was really
a squirrel fur slipper.
It's because the word
squirrel (first attested
in 1327 from Anglo-
Norman) is so ludicrous,
so comical, and I can't
stand when people laugh
at my poems when they
are meant to be serious.
So fuck you, squirrel, fuck you.

Welcome

Welcome to *Memory Air.*
We fly to everywhere
you have forgotten.

The older you are,
the more destinations
we fly you to.

Or if you prefer,
you may zoom
non-stop to the womb.

On the Plane

to San Francisco, a black
dude came down the aisle.
He had a mustache and
a few patches of beard.
He had a black hat with
a big brim and a wilted
feather. He had a steel
chain made of big clanky
links around his neck.
He had a black leather
vest with steel bosses.
I looked up. "You're
a famous musician," I said.
"I recognize you." He
looked down. He blinked.
His eyes were slightly
bloodshot. "Uh, yeah," he
said. "A little. How you
doin', man? Nice to meet
you." "Same here," I said.

In the Row

in front of me,
a little boy
was looking out
the window
when his mother said,
"Do you know why
the sky is blue?"
"Because god
has blue eyes?"
"Well, no," laughed
the mother. "But
that will do for now."

Clouds

They look the same
from up here

above them,
except there are

more of them,
and they have less to say.

The Wasatch

On the trail,
lightning and thunder.

The gods were angry,
but not with me,

for that is not
my kind of flattery.

Bridal Veil Falls

It is named for
an Indian legend.

Ah, the best kind.

Utah Red Rock

If I lived here,
I would have to do
a lot better than this.
Fortunately,
I'm a tourist.

Arches

We all succumb.
Some resist longer.

Some murmur, "No," louder.
But in time, we all succumb.

We all succumb to time
in time.

Two Old Indians

"They sound like chattering crows,
don't they?" said one.
"Yeah, but I understand crows.
I don't understand that tribe,"
said the other.

The Woman of My Dreams

She was waiting in front of the post
office. She was the woman of my dreams.
I came out and saw her. "Hello," I said.
She giggled. "Oh, I'm sorry," she said.
"I thought you were someone else."
"I am someone else," I said. She giggled
again. "I'm stalking you," she said.
She touched my arm. "Please continue,"
I said. "I'm very stalkable." She started
to walk with me. "But my wife is waiting
in the car over there," I said. "Have a nice
day," she said. She walked away to her car.
"Okay," I said. She looked back at me.
I looked back at her. She must have
stopped stalking me. That was months ago.
I haven't seen her since. At least I met her,
the woman of my dreams. That's more
than most men my age can say.

Part II:

Ghazal-Sonnets

Fire

"When one burns one's bridges, what a very nice fire
 it makes," is a great quote by the Welsh poet Dylan Thomas.

"Just as a candle cannot burn without fire,
men cannot live without a spiritual life," said the Buddha.

"Education is not the filling of a pail, but the lighting of a fire."
This was said by the Irish poet William Butler Yeats.

John Wesley, founder of Methodism, said, "Catch on fire
and people will come for miles to see you burn."

Earth is the only known planet with fire.
There isn't enough oxygen anywhere else.

Written in 1938, "I Don't Want to Set the World on Fire"
is a pop song recorded most notably by The Ink Spots.

> So, Solonche, aren't you going to fix the format of this
>   ghazal on fire?
> Yes. Here goes. Stand back. *Ready fire. Aim fire. Fire fire.*

Stone

He's not my savior, but I like a lot of things Jesus said.
One is, "Let him who is without sin cast the first stone."

I never thought I'd quote Keith Richards (even use his name in a
    poem),
but "you've got the sun, you've got the moon, and you've got the
    Rolling Stones."

"I know not with what weapons World War III will be fought," said
    Albert Einstein
more seriously, "but World War IV will be fought with sticks and
    stones."

"Stoned" is borrowed from older expressions like "stone drunk" or
    "stone cold."
This is consistent with the now familiar image of the supine
    lifeless "stoner."

In England in 1389 a royal statute fixed the standard unit of wool
    at 14 pounds.
It is still used for people and large animals and is called a "stone."

There are many forms of inhumane execution in the world.
Perhaps the most barbaric is from the bible, death by stoning.

> So, Solonche, any last words to share with us about this
>   interesting word?
> Carve *He cast a cold eye on life, on death but with a
>   twinkle in it* on my headstone.

Moon

The third full moon in a month that has two is called a "blue
    moon."
A moon more than half full but not fully illuminated is a gibbous
    moon.

The full moon nearest the autumnal equinox is known as the
    "harvest moon."
A popular 1900's song has the words, "Oh, shine on, shine on
    harvest moon."

Twelve American males are the only people to have ever set foot
    on the moon.
In the 1950s, scientists wanted to detonate a nuclear bomb on the
    moon.

"There is nothing you can see that is not a flower," said Basho in
    moonlight.
"There is nothing you can think that is not the moon."

There are many proverbs from all over the world about the moon.
From Russia comes *As long as the sun shines one does not ask for
    the moon.*

From China comes *One's shadow grows larger than life when
    admired by the light of the moon.*
From Africa comes *If you cry because you miss the sun, your tears
    will not let you see the moon.*

So, Solonche, what on earth inspired this ghazal on the moon?
This ghazal was inspired by the Eternal Her, the Triple Goddess
    of the Moon.

Night

South African writer J.M. Coetzee won the Nobel Prize for
    Literature.
Among many things he said is, "The barbarians come out at night."

The writer Elie Wiesel won the Nobel Prize for Peace.
His most famous work is the novel *Night.*

Here is a line from Act I, Scene 2 of *Hamlet:*
"In the dead vast and middle of the night."

Emily Dickinson wrote many enigmatic poems.
The most enigmatic is (269) "Wild nights—Wild nights!"

Like Emily Dickinson, Robert Frost also lived in Amherst, Mass.
One of his best-known poems is the sonnet "Acquainted with the
    Night."

In Greek mythology, Nyx was the goddess of night.
In Hindu mythology, Ratri was the goddess of night.

        So, Solonche, do you have any advice to impart tonight?
        Yes, the poet was right who said to never write at night.

Rose

Over the centuries, England was involved in many wars.
The one with the best name is "The War of the Roses."

Robert Burns is the national poet of Scotland.
His most famous poem is "A Red, Red Rose."

There are many fine straight bourbon whiskeys.
One of the best (Lawrenceburg, Kentucky, 1888) is Four Roses.

There have been many songs with rose in the title.
The best is in French, Edith Piaf's "La vie en rose."

The best known quote about a rose, I suppose,
is Gertrude Stein's "A rose is a rose is a rose."

In a review, Harpo Marx called it "no worse than a bad cold."
It was the 1920s stage play by Anne Nichols, *Abie's Irish Rose.*

    So, Solonche, do you have one more fact for us about a rose?
    My mother-in-law drank, smoked and swore, so I called her
      Black Rose.

Window

Window originates from the Old Norse 'vindauga', from 'vindr—
   wind' and 'auga—eye'.
There are many types of windows, but my favorite is the stained
   glass window.

Before glass, windows were made of paper, cloth, flattened animal
   horn or thin slices of marble.
Only in the early 17th century did glass become common in
   windows.

The average home in the United States has eight windows.
The tallest building in the world, the Burj Khalifa, in Dubai has
   34,348 windows.

At one point, homes in Amsterdam were taxed based on the
   number and size of their windows.
Steve Wozniak said, "Never trust a computer you can't throw out a
   window."

On November 10, 1983, Bill Gates introduced Microsoft Windows.
I am writing this ghazal using a recent version (10?) of Windows.

The playwright George Bernard Shaw had a merciless wit.
He said Keats was the type of young man who wrote "casement"
   rather than "window."

      So, Solonche, what do you see now looking out the window?
      It is dark, so I see myself looking out the mirror of the
         window

Crow

Crow comes from Old English *crawe,* which is held to be imitative
   of the bird's cry.
There's an Indian tribe whose name is Apsaruke that we call the
   Crow.

The birds with the biggest brain-to-body size ratios are the crows.
Making and using tools is a specialty of the New Caledonian
   crows.

Because they hold a grudge, never make an enemy of a crow.
According to the OED, a *murder* is the correct term for a group of
   crows.

In Babylon, the 13th month of the year was named for the crow.
In China, the messengers of the faerie queen His-Wang-Mu are
   crows.

For Mayans, the messenger of the god of lightning and thunder is
   the crow.
In Norse mythology, Wotan is known as the god with the crows.

According to Ovid, it was white until Apollo turned it into a black
   crow.
For the Tlingit Indians, the main divine character is the crow.

   So, Solonche, that's quite a ghazal. Aren't you going to crow?
   I'm too modest for that, but neither am I going to eat crow.

Gray

I do not care much for the poetry of the 18th century.
But I like "An Elegy Written in a Country Church Yard" by
    Thomas Gray.

Americans spell it "gray" whereas the British spell it "grey."
Earl Grey tea is named after Charles Grey, 2nd Earl of Grey.

The United States navy paints all its ships "battleship gray."
Since it's undyed wool, monks and friars wear robes of gray.

The favorite background for El Greco and Rembrandt was gray.
The American Civil War is also known as the War of the Blue and
    the Gray.

When mixed with 6% yellow, gray is warm gray.
When mixed with 6% blue, gray is cool gray.

Women factory workers in 19th century Paris were called
    "grisettes."
Andre Gide said, "The color of truth is gray."

    So, Solonche, anything more in this gray area to say?
    Not now. Let's wait (it won't be long) until I'm old and gray.

Sun

Because he died by refusing to breathe, Diogenes is my favorite
    philosopher.
He famously told Alexander not to stand between him and the sun.

And, "The sun, too, shines into cesspools and is not polluted."
The closest thing to a perfect sphere so far observed is the sun.

Osiris, Apollo, and Balder are all personifications of the sun.
Jonah, Cain, and Noah are all related to the rising and resting of
    the sun.

The Japanese flag is the rising sun.
Namibia, Argentina, Uruguay, Bangladesh, Taiwan, Rwanda all
    show the sun.

A hit song by The Beatles from 1969 is "Here Comes the Sun."
A hit song by The Doors from 1968 is "Waiting for the Sun."

A hit song by Lou Reed is "Ride into the Sun."
My favorite, by The Animals, is "The House of the Rising Sun."

        So, Solonche, got one more of these before we're done?
        I was born under the moon, but I wish to die in the sun.

White

The lightest color, the opposite of black, is white.
As a symbol of purity, priestesses in Egypt and Rome wore white.

As a symbol of citizenship, Roman togas were white.
The royal color of the kings of France was white.

In many Asian cultures, the symbol of mourning is white.
The Inuit language has seven different words for white.

The brightest white paint available is titanium white.
Fluorescent chemicals in detergent make clothing whiter than
 white.

The first child born to the Pilgrims (1620-1704) was Peregrine.
In the 1990 US Census, the 14th ranked surname was White.

A police car (squad car) is often called a black and white.
The greatest films have been shot in black and white.

 So, Solonche, do you have another line of white to enlighten
  us with?
 Sure, for light summer drinking, try Ommegang Witte or
  Allagash White.

Eagle

The common name for large birds of prey of the
   family Accipitridae is "eagle."
The word comes from the Latin, aquila meaning "black eagle."

In golf, two under par (soars higher than a birdie) is called an
   eagle.
Benjamin Franklin wanted the wild turkey to be America's bird,
   not the bald eagle.

An ancient symbol in heraldry and vexillology is the double-
   headed eagle.
Bill Clinton said, "You can put wings on a pig, but you don't make
   it an eagle."

"Hotel California" is probably the most famous song by The
   Eagles.
The world's smallest eagle (500 grams) is the South Nicobar
   Serpent-eagle.

The world's largest eagle is the Philippine or the great monkey-
   eating eagle.
The largest eagle known to have existed (230 kg/510 lbs) was the
   Haast's eagle.

I live near Tomahawk Lake which is home to a nesting pair of bald
   eagles.
The Aetos Dios, Zeus's messenger and animal companion, was a
   giant golden eagle.

   So, Solonche, wouldn't you like to soar like one of those
      eagles?
   I was a Boy Scout once, but I quit long before the rank of
      Eagle.

World

The Proto-Germanic for "age of man" is the origin of the word
    "world."
Just before he's killed, Jimmy Cagney says, "Look, ma, I'm on top
    of the world."

Speaking of movies, many have titles that include the word
    "world."
One (plus bad remake) is based on the novel by H.G. Welles, *The
    War of the Worlds.*

There's a film that featured just about every comedian in the world.
Directed by Stanley Kramer (1963), it was *It's a Mad, Mad, Mad,
    Mad World.*

But a much funnier movie (1981) is Mel Brooks' *History of the
    World.*
Another comedy that did well as the box office (1992) is *Wayne's
    World.*

A lousy film version (1998) of a great novel (1931) by Aldous
    Huxley was *Brave New World.*
Louis Armstrong topped the UK Singles Chart (1967) with *What a
    Wonderful World.*

The flat Babylonian *Imago Mundi* (ca. 6th c. BCE) is thought to be
    the first map of the world.
It was the Greeks who assumed a spherical earth for making their
    maps of the world.

    So, Solonche, other than books and movies, what do you
        want to say about the world?
    For all the world, I want to say something memorable,
        really out of this world.

Whiskey

My favorite type of distilled alcoholic beverage is "whisky" or
  "whiskey."
The word is an anglicisation of the Classical Gaelic word
  uisce (or *uisge*) meaning "water."

Both Ireland and Scotland claim to have given birth to whiskey.
A currency used during the American Revolutionary War was
  whiskey.

Water plus 51% malted barley with 40% alcohol made in Scotland
  is Scotch whiskey.
Water plus 51% corn mash with 40% alcohol made in America is
  bourbon whiskey.

By law in the U.S. whiskey made from a mash of at least 51% rye
  is rye whiskey.
Water plus malted cereals with 40% alcohol made in Ireland is Irish
  whiskey.

Japanese whisky is closer to Scotch than to any other kind of
  whiskey.
 "My God, so much I like to drink Scotch that sometimes I think
  my name is Igor Stra-whiskey."

Ernest Hemingway: "Never delay kissing a pretty girl or opening a
  bottle of whiskey."
William Faulkner:"…the tools I need for my trade are paper,
  tobacco, food, and a little whisky."

    So, Solonche, which whiskey would it take for you to belt
  out one more on whiskey?
    Just this one I'm drinking now, Jim Beam Straight Kentucky
  Bourbon Whiskey.

Dream

The word "dream" comes from the Middle English word "dreme."
My favorite Shakespeare comedy is *A Midsummer Night's Dream.*

The structure of the atom came to Niels Bohr in a dream.
The structure of the benzene molecule came to August Kekulé in a
  dream.

The Theory of Relativity came to Einstein after a vivid dream.
Mendeleev arranged the table of the 63 known (1869) elements in
  a dream.

Mary Shelley's famous novel *Frankenstein* was inspired by a
  dream.
The plot of *Dr. Jekyll and Mr. Hyde* came to R.L. Stevenson in an
  opium dream.

The famous poem "Kubla Khan" came to S.T. Coleridge in an
  opium dream.
An influential book (1899) by Sigmund Freud is *The Interpretation
  of Dreams.*

Carl Jung (1875-1960) broke with Freud over their differing views
  on dreams.
Edgar Allan Poe said, "All that we see or seem is but a dream
  within a dream."

> So, Solonche, la la la la la la la la la la la la life is but a
>   dream?
> I wish it were, for then death, too, would be but a dream.

Yesterday

The word comes from the Old English equivalent of *yester + day*.
The star of the film *Solid Gold Cadillac* was (1921-1965) Judy
    Holliday.

I forgot *Adam's Rib, Bells Are Ringing* and *Born Yesterday*.
The greatest female jazz singer was (1915-1959) Billie Holiday.

The Beatles song that topped the US charts in 1965 is *Yesterday*.
Lincoln: "I do not think much of a man who is not wiser today than
    he was yesterday."

Dale Carnegie: "Remember, today is the tomorrow you worried
    about yesterday."
Don Marquis: "Procrastination is the art of keeping up with
    yesterday."

Jiddu Krishnamurti: "Why does the brain retain the memory of the
    hurt from yesterday?"
Walter de La Mare: "Do diddle di do, Poor Jim Jay/Got stuck fast
    In Yesterday." *

Aristophanes: "Today things are better than yesterday."
Dalai Lama: "Not only can I not recall my previous lives,
    sometimes I can't recall yesterday."

      So, Solonche, how are the sales of *Tomorrow, Today and*
        Yesterday?
      Khalil Gibran: "For life goes not backward, nor tarries with
        yesterday." **

*My favorite.
**Sorry.

Word

The word *word* comes from Old English and from the Proto-
   Germanic *wurda.*
Chinese proverb: "If you wish to know the mind of a man, listen to
   his words."

Confucius: "A gentleman would be ashamed should his deeds not
   match his words."
Pythagoras: "Silence is better than unmeaning words."

Moliere: "I live on good soup, not on fine words."
Ludwig van Beethoven: "Music comes to me more readily than
   words."

Mauve is Nabakov's favorite word.
Edith Piaf: "I want to make people cry even when they don't
   understand my words."

A four-letter word is another name for a swear word.
A saying used all the time is, "A picture is worth a thousand
   words."

Hamlet: (*The Tragedy of Hamlet, Prince of Denmark II,* ii, 210)
   "Words, words, words."
One of my students: "Poetry expresses what we cannot say in
   words."

   So, Solonche, tell us, what's the good word?
   I couldn't tell you, so I'd rather let this ghazal have the last
      word.

King

King is an Old English contraction of *cyning* ("king, ruler") from
  Proto-Germanic *kuningaz*.
One of the great American blues musicians is B.B. King.

One of the great American tennis champs is Billie Jean King.
One of the great American civil rights leaders is Martin Luther
  King, Jr.

Elvis Presley, one of the great American singers, is known as "The
  King."
A 1938 movie about the French poet Francois Villon (Ronald
  Colman) is *If I Were King.*

A 1975 movie based on a Rudyard Kipling novella is *The Man
  Who Would Be King.*
A movie (Disney) and a Broadway musical (Elton John) is *The
  Lion King.*

A popular American author who has written 60 books is Stephen
  King.
In chess the most powerful piece on the board is the queen, not the
  king.

Mark Twain: "Sometimes I wish we could hear of a country that's
  out of kings."
Moliere: "Grammar, which knows how to control even kings."

     So, Solonche, have one more move in this ghazal on king?
     Later, right now I'm reading Tennyson's great poem *Idylls
       of the King.*

Story

Middle English *storie,* from Anglo-French *estoire, estorie,* from
    Latin *historia.*
A fanciful or unbelievable tale is a "cock and bull story."

Audrey Hepburn starred in the 1959 film (Fred Zinnemann dir.)
    The Nun's Story.
A computer animated film nominated for three Academy Awards
    (1995) is *Toy Story.*

Anton Chekhov was a great playwright as well as a great writer of
    short stories.
Edgar Allan Poe is regarded as the inventor of the detective story.

Alice Munro won the 2013 Nobel Prize in Literature for her
    collections of short stories.
Having a word count of fewer than 7,500 words is the definition of
    a sci-fi short story.

Isak Dinesen: "All sorrows can be borne if you can put them into a
    story."
Leo Tolstoy: "Happiness is an allegory, unhappiness a story."

Carl Jung: "The reason for evil in the world is that people are not
    able to tell their stories."
Bertolt Brecht: "People who understand everything get no stories."

    So, Solonche, don't be coy. What's the story?
    Get your tissues, pull up a chair and sit down 'cause it's a
        long sob story.

Time

Before 900; (noun) Middle English; Old English *tīma;* cognate
    with Old Norse *tīmi.*
Oscar Wilde: "Punctuality is the thief of time."

Benjamin Disraeli: "Time is precious, but truth is more precious
    than time."
William Blake: "Eternity is in love with the productions of time."

A book I never hope to understand is Stephen Hawking's *A Brief
    History of Time.*
Marcus Aurelius: "The memory of everything is very soon
    overwhelmed in time."

Seneca: "The part of life we really live is small, for all the rest of
    existence is merely time."
One of the greatest lyric poems (Andrew Marvell) begins, "Had we
    but world enough and time."

Anon.: "Since it cannot ever be returned, how can one say one
    lives on borrowed time?"
G.K. Chesterton: "One of the great disadvantages of hurry is that it
    takes such a long time."

Francis Bacon: "A man that is young in years may be old in hours
    if he have lost no time."
Julian Barnes: "Art is the whisper of history, heard above the noise
    of time."

      So, Solonche, you rascal you, what is it this time?
      It? Sure, I'll come out with it. It's only a matter of time.

Heart

Middle English *herte,* from Old English *heorte* ("heart"),
    from Proto-Germanic *hertô*.
My favorite pizza toppings are mushrooms, black olives, and
    artichoke hearts.

"The Luck of Roaring Camp" is a famous story by the writer
    (1836-1902) Bret Harte.
When Shelley drowned and was cremated, the only organ not to
    burn was his heart.

The Book of Exodus is very confusing regarding who hardens
    pharaoh's heart.
My favorite story by Poe is (hark! louder! louder! louder!) "The
    Tell-Tale Heart."

Beth Henley won a Pulitzer Prize (1981) for her play *Crimes of the
    Heart.*
A great country music song by Hank Williams (1952) is "Your
    Cheatin' Heart."

Franklin: "The heart of a fool is in his mouth, the mouth of a wise
    man in his heart."
Einstein: "Few are those who see with their own eyes and feel with
    their own hearts."

Marcel Proust: "Love is space and time measured by the heart."
George Sand: "The artist's vocation is to send light into the human
    heart."

> So, Solonche, can you recite this heart ghazal by heart?
> From the bottom of my heart, I say to you, heart to heart,
>   have a heart.

Blue

My favorite kind of music is Mississippi Delta blues.
My favorite blues song (1914) is W.C. Handy's "St. Louis Blues."

Billie Holiday, Ethel Waters, and Ray Charles all recorded "Am I
    Blue?"
Fats Waller composed (listen to Louis Armstrong's recording) of
    "Black and Blue."

As a progressive Democrat, I prefer states that are blue.
My favorite flag is France's red, white, and blue (rouge, blanc, et
    bleu).

My favorite breed of cat is the Russian Blue (aka the Archangel
    Blue).
Bluetick coonhounds, as well as other hound breeds, are often
    named *Blue.*

Down at the marsh off Farmingdale Road lives a heron, great and
    blue.
My favorite color for a wool blazer (with khaki pants) is navy blue.

My favorite color of a woman's eyes (blonde, brunette or redhead)
    is baby blue.
The Oakland A's had a pretty good pitcher (W209-L161) named
    Vida Blue.

        So, Solonche, why is the sky blue?
        Wow, that came out of the blue, and now I, too, am out of
            the blue.

Apple

From Middle English *appel,* from Old English *æppel* from Proto-
Germanic *aplaz*.
The very first word Emily, our daughter we adopted from China,
    spoke was "apple."

The fruit of the Tree of Knowledge was a pomegranate not an
    apple.
This means Steve Jobs should have called his company
    Pomegranate instead of Apple.

Grown around the world are over 7,500 varieties of apples.
The only apple native to the United States is the crabapple.

Johnny Appleseed planted apple trees for hard cider, not for eating
    apples.
Malusdomesticaphobia is the fear of apples.

A trench mortar used by the British in World War I was the "Toffee
    Apple."
For two days I worked at an orchard picking (on a fucking 20 foot
    ladder!) apples.

New York City (or only Manhattan) is also known as "The Big
    Apple."
At New York University, I knew a girl from Montreal, Canada,
    named Pomey.

    So, Solonche, how do you like them apples?
    I like all them apples, but the only one I ever loved is the
        last apple.

Happy

Merriam-Webster says, "favored by luck or fortune" is the first
   definition of *happy.*
It also says, "feeling or showing pleasure" is the first "Kids
   Definition" of *happy.*

"On cloud nine" first appeared in The Oxnard Press-Courier
   (1946) to mean happy.
Emerson: "For every minute you are angry you lose sixty seconds
   of happiness."

An interesting book (1930) by Bertrand Russell is *The Conquest of
   Happiness.*
Dostoevsky: "Man only likes to count his troubles; he doesn't
   calculate his happiness."

Anne Frank *(The Diary of a Young Girl):* "Whoever is happy will
   make others happy."
Stendhal: "There are as many styles of beauty as there are visions
   of happiness."

The Unabridged Journals of Sylvia Plath: "Is anyone anywhere
   happy?"
Jane Austen *(Emma):* "You must be the best judge of your own
   happiness."

The guiding philosophy of the government of Bhutan is GNH
   (Gross National Happiness).
Anton Chekhov: "Even in Siberia there is happiness."

> So, Solonche, what happened to life, liberty, and the pursuit
>   of happiness?
> Well, to tell the truth, life and liberty are fine, but I was
>   outrun by happiness.

Wisdom

Middle English, from Old English, from *Proto-Indo-European root word weid.*
The chief in *One Flew over the Cuckoo's Nest* is the epitome of wisdom.

Aristotle: "Knowing yourself is the beginning of all wisdom."
Socrates: "Wonder is the beginning of wisdom."

Chinese proverb: "Calling things by their right names is the beginning of wisdom."
Jefferson: "Honesty is the first chapter of the book wisdom."

Thomas Gray: "Where ignorance is bliss (Eton College) 'tis folly to be wise."
The name of our species, Homo sapiens sapiens means "man the wise."

Franklin: "Early to bed and early to rise makes a man healthy, wealthy, and wise."
Francis Bacon: "Silence is the sleep that nourishes wisdom."

Robert Frost: "A poem begins in delight and ends in wisdom."
E. E. Cummings: "Kisses are a better fate than wisdom."

> So, Solonche, please, what are your final words of wisdom?
> Just read my *shit* ghazal (next page) for its wit and wisdom.

Shit

Noun: Middle English *shit,* from Old English *scite;* akin to Old
English—*scītan.*
Verb: alteration of earlier *shite,* from Middle English *shiten,*
from Old English—*scītan.*

Urban Dictionary: One of the most popular swear/cuss/curse
words/profanities is *shit.*
Mel Brooks: "I've been accused of vulgarity. I say that's bullshit."

Ernest Hemingway: "The first draft of anything is shit."
Marcus Aurelius *(Meditations):* "He is so rich, he has no room to
shit."

HITs, Hist, Tish, hist, hist-, hist., hits, iths, sith, this, tish are
anagrams of *shit.*
T-shirt (Made in India): "Women Don't Owe You Shit"

https://internetofshit.net/
https://www.instagram.com/cakes.and.shit/?hl=en

A great poem by Galway Kinnell is "Holy Shit."
"An In-Depth Analysis of a Piece of Shit" (December 20, 2012)
No shit!

> So, Solonche, what the hell is all this stupid shit?
> I just wanted to get it together, you know, all my stupid
> shit.

Life

Middle English *lif,* from Old English *līf;* akin to Old
English *libban.*
A beloved Christmas movie (1946) starring James Stewart is *It's
a Wonderful Life.*

Marion Montgomery (1934-2002) was the first to record
Sinatra's hit (1966) *That's Life.*
Many famous people appeared on the NBC program (1952-1961)
This is Your Life.

Doubleday, Page & Co. published (1903) Helen Keller's
autobiography *The Story of My Life.*
A weekly, then monthly, magazine (1936-1972) known for its
photography is *life.*

The magazine started by the Boy Scouts of America in 1911 is
Boy's Life.
Mark Twain: "Good friends, good books, and a sleepy conscience
is the ideal life."

Jonathan Swift said (I was surprised) "May you live everyday of
your life."
E.E. Cummings said (I was not surprised) "Unbeing dead isn't
being alive."

Steve Jobs: "Your time is limited, so don't waste it living someone
else's life."
Omar Khayyam: "Be happy for this moment, for this moment is
your life."

So, Solonche, do you have a new lease on life?
No, I'm holding on to the old one for dear life.

Beer

Probably a 6th century West Germanic monastic borrowing of
    Vulgar Latin *biber*.
Archaeologists in Israel have found the residues of 13,000 year old
    Natufian beer.

The sponsor of the Brooklyn Dodgers was Schaefer (scoreboard *h*
    and *e* lit up) Beer.
The sponsor of the New York Giants *(Have a Knick!)* was
    Knickerbocker Beer.

The sponsor of the New York Yankees *(A Ballantine blast!)* was
    Ballantine Beer.
Plato: "He was a wise man who invented beer."

Ancient Egyptian saying: "The mouth of a perfectly happy man is
    filled with beer."
Henry Lawson, Australian poet: "Beer makes you feel the way you
    ought to feel without beer."

Washington Irving: "They who drink beer will think beer."
Sam Adams: "Let no man thirst for good beer."

Anne Sexton: "God has a brown voice, as soft and full as beer."
Homer Simpson: "I would kill everyone in this room for a drop of
    sweet beer."

    So, Solonche, what do you say we go for a beer?
    Only if it's 1964 and you're Celeste Yarnall, Miss
        Rheingold the Dry Beer.

Song

Old English *sang,* of Germanic origin; related to Dutch *zang* and
    German *Sang.*
Male hedonistic pleasures are summarized as wine, women, and
    song.

Speaking of pleasures, in my time I've heard many a siren song.
I'll write a song and dance ghazal next, but in this one I have to say
    "a dance and a song."

I can't think of anything I've bought or sold for a song.
Rolling Stone Magazine ranks Bob Dylan's "Like a Rolling Stone"
    the #1 song.

Michael Jackson's "Thriller" is ranked the #1 pop song.
W.C. Handy's "Memphis Blue" is the greatest blues song.

"Hoochie Coochie Man" by Muddy Waters is the greatest blues
    song.
B.B. King's "The Thrill Is Gone" is the greatest blues song.

"I'd Rather Go Blind" by Etta James is the greatest blues song.
Howlin Wolf's "Smokestack Lightning" is the greatest blues song.

      So, Solonche, you do know that you need one more song?
      Yes, I do know I need one more song, so here is my swan
        song.

Dance

Middle English: from Old French dancer (verb), dance (noun), of
  unknown origin.
Terpsichore (the most beautiful of the nine) is the Greek muse of
  dance.

As I promised, now I can quote the correct idiom of a song and a
  dance.
I never went to my high school prom because I didn't know how to
  dance.

One of the biggest hit songs (The Bee Gees) is "You Should Be
  Dancing."
The debut (2008) single (Grammy nominated 2009) by Lady Gaga
  was "Just Dance."

The samba of Brazil is the world's most popular folk dance.
Baladi is a form of Egyptian belly dance, a truly hypnotic dance.

The hora is a popular Israeli circle dance.
Popular in South Africa is the gumboot (they wear Wellingtons)
  dance.

Clogging is the official Kentucky and North Carolina state dance.
Minnesota is the only state that has no official state dance.

> So, Solonche, will you, won't you, will you, won't you,
>   won't you join the dance?
> Oh, someday, one day, maybe Sunday, I may, I mean, I
>   might join the dance.

Holy

Old English *hālig,* of Germanic origin; related to Dutch and
    German *heilig.*
William Shakespeare, *All's Well That Ends Well:* "Love is holy."

In the first season (1966) of *Batman,* Robin said 356 phrases with
    holy.
The room in a synagogue where only the rabbi may enter is the
    holy of holies.

The exclamation used by Captain Marvel to mean *Wow!* is *Holy
    Moley!*
The trademark expression of Yankee broadcaster Phil Rizzuto
    (1917-2007) was *Holy cow!*

In the New Testament, "set apart" is the definition of holiness.
In the Old Testament, the connection to God's perfection was
    holiness.

Sapta (seven) Puri (town) are the seven cities in India considered
    the most holy.
In Buddhism, Bodh Gaya (where Buddha attained Enlightenment)
    is the holiest.

In the Shinto religion of Japan, The Grand Shrine of Ise is
    considered the most holy.
Of the sacred sites for Muslims, The Ka'ba in Mecca, Saudi
    Arabia, is the most holy.

>   So, Solonche, you atheist, what, if anything, do you
>   consider holy?
>   Like the other atheist above said, "Love is holy."

Earth

Old English *eorthe,* of Germanic origin; related to Dutch *aarde* and
    German *Erde.*
This is not at all the same as the ghazal on the *world,* which is
    different from the earth.

Gustave Mahler wrote (1908) a magnificent song cycle called *Das
    Lied von der Erde.*
The only planet in our solar system not named after a Greek or
    Roman god is the earth.

The densest planet in the solar system is the earth.
For 146 years, the Ringling Bros. Circus was "The Greatest Show
    on Earth."

The only place in the solar system with water in all three states is
    the earth.
The only planet in the solar system with tectonic plates is the earth.

Pearl S. Buck's novel that won the Pulitzer Prize (1932) is *The
    Good Earth.*
Archimedes said, "Give me a place to stand and a lever and I will
    move the Earth."

A song by George and Ira Gershwin from the musical *Oh, Kay!*
    (1926) is "Heaven on Earth."
Songs by The Platters (1956) and by Britney Spears (2007) are
    both "Heaven on Earth."

    So, Solonche, out with it, what do you really want to say,
        what on earth?
    By our foolish and selfish behavior we humans are
        creating hell on earth.

Water

Old English *wæter* (Germanic from an Indo-European root shared
  by Russian *voda*).
Among the many idioms with water is, "Come hell or high water."

Another good one is, "Don't throw the baby out with the
  bathwater."
Benjamin Franklin: "When the well's dry, we know the worth of
  water."

Paul Simon's biggest hit single (1970) is "Bridge over Troubled
  Water."
The first of the two #1 hit singles (1975) by the Doobie Brothers is
  "Black Water."

Third on the Top 100 Western songs of all time (Bob Nolan, 1936)
  is "Clear Water."
W.H. Auden: "Thousands have lived without love, not one without
  water."

My favorite book (1965) by Kurt Vonnegut is *God Bless You, Mr.
  Rosewater.*
W.C. Fields: "Say anything that you like about me except that I
drink water."

Ha, ha. You must see his short film (1946) "The Day I Drank a
  Glass of Water."
Laurel and Hardy's final short film (1935) is "Thicker than Water,"

> So, Solonche, you must be thirsty, so would you like a glass
>   of water?
> I am thirsty, but don't bring your damn water near my glass
>   of giggle water.

Poetry

Middle English, Old French poete, via Latin from Greek poētēs, variant of poiētēs 'maker, poet'.

Dickinson: "If I feel physically as if the top of my head were taken off, I know that is poetry."

Poe: "All religion is simply evolved out of fraud, fear, greed, imagination, and poetry."

Johann Wolfgang von Goethe: "Personality is everything in art and poetry."

W. Somerset Maugham: "The crown of literature is poetry."

Michael Eric Dyson: "Hip-hop is about the brilliance of pavement poetry."

Virginia Woolf: "The best prose is that which is most full of poetry."

John Cage: "I have nothing to say, I am saying it, and that is poetry."

Gilbert K. Chesterton: "All slang is a metaphor, and all metaphor is poetry."

Howard Nemerov: "A lot happens by accident in poetry."

John Donne: "I am two fools, I know, for loving, and for saying so in whining poetry."

Carol Ann Duffy: "I still read Donne, particularly his love poems."

So, Solonche, can't you stop quoting and say something original about poetry?

Solonche: "They think they wax poetic, but most poets these days wane poetic."

Last

Old English *latost* (adverb) 'after all others in a series', Old
   English *lǣstan* (verb).
Leo Durocher (about the 1946 New York Giants): "Nice guys
   finish last."

Matthew 20:16 (KJV): "So the last shall be first, and the first last."
Vanessa Williams was nominated for a Grammy (1993) for "Save
   the Best for Last."

The tenth track on Barbra Streisand's album *Emotion* (1984) is
   "Here We Are at Last."
The Urban Dictionary: "A male that cannot outlast a woman
   during sex" is a *Never Last.*

Samurai, Action Hero, Emperor, of the Mohicans, Tango in Paris
   are all movies with *Last.*
John Heywood's book of proverbs (1546) is the source of "he who
   laughs last…"

When Gustav Mahler died (May 18, 1911), "Mozart" was the word
   he spoke last.
When Winston Churchill died (Jan. 24, 1965), the words "I'm
   bored with it all" were his last.

The words, "I'll finally get to see Marilyn," were Joe Dimaggio's
   last.
The words "Last words are for fools who haven't said enough"
   were Karl Marx's last.

   So, Solonche, what do you want to say before you
      breathe your last?
   I want to say one thing—just one thing—that will last and
      last.

Part III

The Wind

The sky is broken into clouds.
The clouds are broken into the children of themselves.

Trying to get out, the wind has broken its neck against
the wall at the end of the world.

The twigs have broken from the branches.
The leaves have broken from the twigs.

The earth is the heart of the sky, and it is breaking.
The world breaks every promise it makes.

It has never been taught to keep them.
Every promise is broken twice, once before and once after.

The earth never breaks its promises.
You can always tell where the wind has been.

It tells you with the song it learns there.
The wind minds its manners.

It knocks—one, two, three times—before it enters your house.
Of all the animals, the wind loves the horses the most.

Of all the birds, the falcon it has yet to conquer.
The stems of the lilies have been broken in half.

The heads of the lilies have been broken off.
The petals of the lilies have been broken away.

The wind is not afraid of the dark.
The wind makes its own way in the world.

The wind whistles while it works.
The wind takes your breath away, then breaks it.

On an Anonymous Japanese Painting

The old man is listening to whatever is happening
to time, and the woman is listening to whatever time
is happening, and the child is listening to the woman,
his mother. The old man carries a nightingale in a cage.
From the way the old man carries himself, from the way he carries
the nightingale as though it were something he was anxious to give
away before he dies, but he has not yet found the right person to
give it to, for a nightingale is not passed without thought to a son
or a daughter as a house, or a sword, or a jewel, as a matter of
course, but is something that may be passed even to a total stranger
one meets on a road if he is worthy, one can tell that the old man is
old enough to wish not to know another winter.

January

"What right do you have," said
the snapping turtle sleeping in
the mud of the lake bed, "to be
thinking of writing a poem about
spring when all I can do is wait
for it under all this cold mud?"
So I apologized to the snapping
turtle and stopped thinking about
writing a poem about spring.

The Waters Are Gone

The waters are gone.
The lake water is frozen over.
The ditch water is frozen.
The marsh water is frozen all around.
Only the wings of the birds are moving.
Only the voices of the birds are calling.
While the water holds its breath.

Sermon on the Balcony

Blessed are the children in the parking lot,
for they shall pick up leaves to give to their fathers.

Blessed are the dogs on the leashes,
for they shall save us from loneliness in old age.

Blessed are the housekeepers,
for they shall prepare the way for our dreaming on clean sheets.

Blessed are the chefs in the kitchens,
for they shall prepare us a feast with the sweat of their brow.

Blessed are the conductors on the trains,
for they shall prepare us the way of our future with names.

Blessed are the drivers of the trains,
for they shall deliver us to where we are going.

Blessed are the employees of Starbucks,
for they shall think abbotancostello is an Italian roast.

Blessed are the fliers of the kites on the rise of the park,
for they shall make us feel like children again who wonder at the
    wind.

Blessed are the fishermen who are hungry in spirit only,
for they in their mercy shall throwback the catch to the water of
    the bay.

Blessed are the homeless,
for they shall reawaken the spirit of our sympathy from its slumber.

Blessed are the personal trainers,
for they shall prepare our body for our ripeness in old age.

Blessed are the therapists,
for they shall prepare our minds for our dementia in old age.

Blessed are the bicyclists,
for they shall leave their spokes coruscating in their wake.

Blessed are the tenders of the bars,
for they shall prepare the way of our daydream, laugh at our joke,
    and nod at our complaint.

Blessed are the poets on the balconies,
for they shall inherit the Word and keep it holy.

Angels

They do not need them for flight,
the wings, but instead
flaunt them for our sake.

We need them to need them,
so we can know how they
vanquish the earth,

how they resist by rising above them,
all the trite temptations
of the world.

The true difference between us
is the face,
without blemish,

without age's crease,
with only that tiny smile,
that tiny seed of wings.

Gorge

Straight lines. Right angles. Symmetry.
Water has learned geometry,
stone, the split, flat flake of crystal,

tree, shrub, weed, the plane's bisections,
to live on ends, on edges well
enough to hold the same seasons

as any soil shoots roots and seize.
And, descending through epochs, we
learn from gouged, gray walls, tilted hall

of the deep past, gauged by this stone
by a stone of indifference until
disgorged, what time's gorged itself on.

What the Poet Said at the Reception after the Reading

To pick up pen and paper, he said,
you must put down yourself first
on the floor under the chair or beside
the dusty corn plant. Your left hand,
he said must, if you are right-handed,
touch the paper to complete the circuit
of the pen and the arm, the circle of
the shoulders and the teeth, for the words
come humming and buzzing through
the teeth and the circle must not be
broken but both hands must be kept
in touch with pen and paper, and you
must keep an eye on yourself, your self
which will try to crawl up your leg and
along your arm and down the pen onto
the paper before you are done. The poet
actually said this nonsense, but he was
a great poet, and he was very drunk, so
we took careful notes and made allowances.

The Practice

A roof. Another. And another. And trees
like hedges beyond them. But the trees
have no roofs, always open to the weather
of the world, the sky's color. In my office,
I open *The Practice of Poetry.* I decide
I need more practice. I close the book,
open the window, put my head out as far as
I can."I need practice," I almost say out loud
to the trees that don't need it, to the sky that
doesn't need it, to the grass that doesn't need it,
to the students passing below who wouldn't
know what the hell I was talking about anyway.
Why doesn't it come as easily, as naturally as
getting leaves? As losing leaves? It's cold. I close
the window. I open the window. I close the window.

The Dark House

In the dark,
the dark house
looks at itself
and wants to leave.

It is darker
in the daylight
when it cannot sleep.
They who live here

are elsewhere,
but they have left
their shadows
in the dark rooms.

The house is lost
in the dark
and does not know
which way to turn.

The darkness wears
the house
like a mask.
What time is it?

What day is it?
What year?
Whose shadows are these?
Only the house is home.

The Dark Lake

What is in
the dark lake?

Fish with
something to hide.

The questionable
pasts of turtles.

Black snakes
with black hearts.

Worse and
the future of worse.

To the Families of 11 Climbers Who Died in a Collapse of an Ice Wall on Mt. Rainier

You say you want to bring them home.
I say do not bring them home.
I say leave them there.
Leave them where they were swept into steep death.
Leave them in peace, and do not steal their mountain sleep.
Leave them, and do not slip them into more familiar ground,
as though the rest belonged to family.
Leave them there, and do not disturb their mountain peace.
Leave them where they cannot fall again, again be buried.
Leave them, for they cannot die again for you.
Leave them, for they cannot be returned to your communities
of ease in life, ease out of life.
Leave them there.
Leave them, and do not steal their mountain death,
most mystical of deaths.
Leave them to their mountain,
the mountain that shouted their names in unison,
the mountain that danced.
Leave them to their mountain, and consider them drowned,
consider them lost at sea.
Leave them to their mountain sleep,
bravest of sleeps.
Leave them to their mountain.
Leave them there,
and do not take their mountain from them, their stone.
Leave them alone.

Cheap Red Wine

1.

One glass of cheap red wine
under a full moon
is equal to two under none.

2.

This cheap red wine is dark
as the cheap red wine-dark sea all right,
but shallow as the cheap red wine-dark rain puddle.

3.

Cheap wine. Once more, fill my
glass? But will I be able
to finish this hai

When the Ice Thaws

When the ice thaws
and the snow melts
and they sluice as one
down the ditches into the
stream and into the lake,
which also is going back
to water again in the warm
sun, my neighbor's septic
awakens. It is pungent in
my nose, and makes me
almost regret it is spring.

The Passenger Jet

The passenger jet
leaves its long broken
contrail straight across
the sky behind as though
it was the dotted line
of the contract
the skywriter will sign.

Hammock

Slowly clouds move white across the sky.
   I am neither sleeping nor awake.
      The world sways. It is balanced on my eye.

      Suddenly, light as light, a butterfly.
   I dream it neither sleeping nor awake.
Its wings swing. They balance on my eye.

Then, liquid as light, a dragonfly.
   I never dreamed it sleeping or awake,
      balanced on the world balanced on my eye.

      Finally, lithe as light, you, lovely wife,
   life's life while life is sleeping and awake,
come to balance on the balance of my.

Linda's Office Supply

I was in Linda's Office Supply.
She was laminating a poem for me.
Never mind why.
That's another story.

A woman came in.
She wanted to buy a scent-free candle.
Linda showed the woman a scent-free candle.
The woman wanted to buy matches.

Linda didn't have matches.
Neither did I.
Linda gave me my laminated poem.
I paid and left.

I was wrong.
It's the same story, not another story.
Linda made nine copies of "Beer Ghazal."
I leave them in the bars I go to with Jim on Saturdays.

I'll be going back to Linda's Office supply for more.
The lamination protects them from beer spills as well as tear spills.
Poems must be beer-proof.
Poems must be tear-proof, especially, especially.

I don't know why the woman needed a scent-free candle and
    matches.
It must have been important whatever it was.
It is the only story we know.
It is the story that involves tears.

O blessings upon you.
O blessings upon whatever it was.
O blessings upon blessings upon blessings upon you.
O Woman with Scent-free Candle Burning, Burning that No Tears
May Extinguish!

Cutty Sark

The jazz musician in the movie drank Cutty Sark.
I'm a sucker for jazz music.
I'm a sucker for movies about jazz musicians.
Weel done, Cutty-sark!
And in an instant all was dark.

I'm a sucker for jazz musicians who drink Scotch.
This one drank a bottle every night.
I'm a sucker for a jazz musician who does that and still makes
    music.
Weel done, Cutty Sark!
And in an instant all was dark.

I wanted to see if I could drink and still make poems.
I found out that I could not.
I found out that I could not drink and still make poems.
Weel done, Cutty-sark!
And in an instant all was dark.

I found out that I wasn't cut out to be maker of poems.
It has taken my whole life.
It has taken my whole life to find out I'm not cut out.
Weel done, Cutty-sark!
And in an instant all was dark.

But it's not too late.
It's not too late to learn to make a poem.
There is still time, still time, still time.
Weel done, Cutty-sark!
And in an instant all was dark.

There is still time, still time, still time.
There is yet time to make a poem, to make but one.
There is still time to be a poet once for all who makes a perfect
    rhyme.
Weel done, Cutty-sark!
And in an instant all was dark.

Photograph by Emily Solonche

About the Author

J.R. Solonche is the author of eighteen books of poetry and co-author of one. He lives in the Hudson Valley.

www.ingramcontent.com/pod-product-compliance
Lightning Source LLC
Chambersburg PA
CBHW022011080426
42733CB00007B/565